COUNTRY HOUSE
LIVING

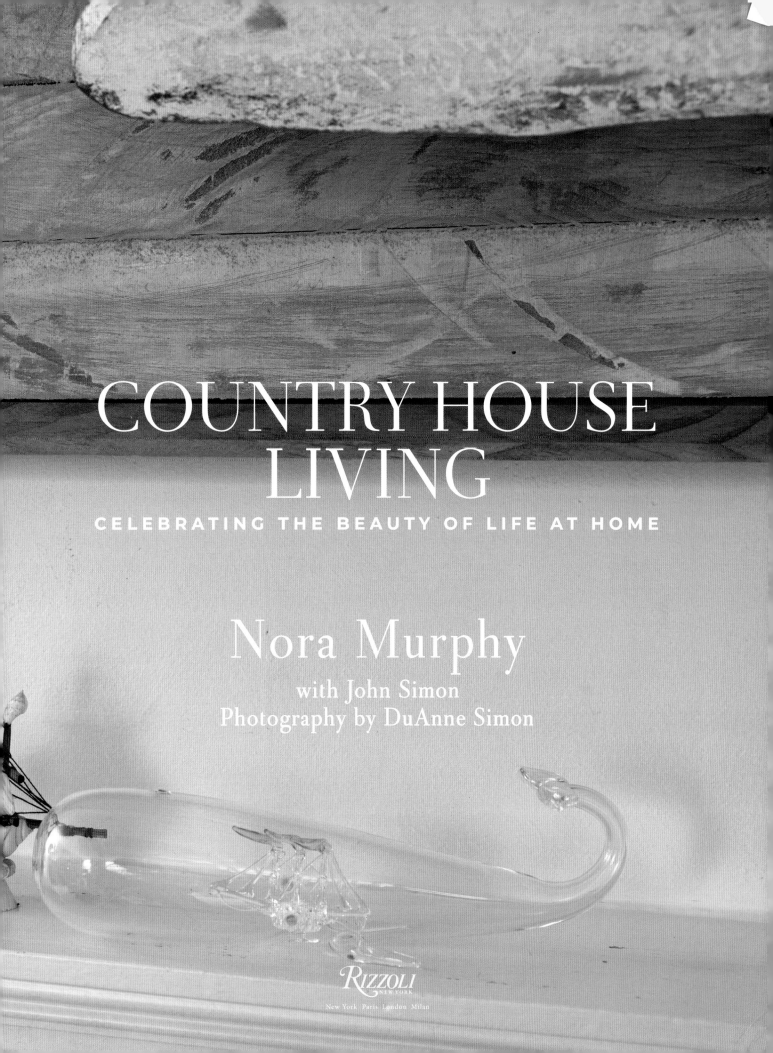

COUNTRY HOUSE LIVING

CELEBRATING THE BEAUTY OF LIFE AT HOME

Nora Murphy

with John Simon
Photography by DuAnne Simon

RIZZOLI
NEW YORK

New York Paris London Milan

With much love I dedicate this book
to my dear friend and photographer
extraordinaire DuAnne Simon for capturing
so beautifully our family's country house life
for over twenty years. Truly a gift.

welcoming 12

elegant 52

timeless 139

graceful 167

joyful 84

soulful 115

artful 197

pastoral 219

introduction

Every country house tells a story. There's the house itself. How it was built, where it exists, everything the house has experienced and lived through. There are the homeowners. Why they chose their home, the journey they took to find it, and the feeling that they create. Country house style is inspired by that feeling. It's about discovering the genuine character of a home, its heartbeat, and making that home a place to be truly, wonderfully lived in.

So, this book, like my first one, is personal. There are stories about how the homeowners came upon their country houses and why they purchased them—stories as varied and fascinating as the homes themselves. It might have been a crazed, whirlwind discovery, or a patient, yearslong search. It might have been a desire to stay close to home, near family and friends, or a yearning to settle in another state or region that intrigued them. For some, the house is an expansive space to showcase their collections or a place to raise their family. For others, like me, buying a house is an opportunity to downsize.

Without a doubt the unsung stars of this book are the homeowners themselves, because without them, we wouldn't have these fascinating homes to be enamored with! They've made country house style personal and written their own stories.

It's funny, people often think that I designed these beautiful homes, but I didn't. These homeowners are their own designers. They have their own styles, and what you see on these pages are their personal visions. Some, like me, have a background in interior design; others not at all. But they all have one thing in common—they know what they like. Each one of these homeowners has embraced country house style and implemented it in their own unique way. Their stories are about creating an environment they love to be in. It's about living a life they love in a home they love.

Interestingly, there is a common thread that weaves through the stories of each of these homes: the collections their owners have thoughtfully, carefully amassed. All seem to feel the thrill of the hunt in unearthing each unique treasure, whether it be in a European village, a church thrift shop, a local antique store, a flea market, a department store clearance sale, or on social media. They keep everything decidedly unfussy and make their love of flora, fauna, and nature a part of their style. They find everyday items and use them in surprising, unexpected ways, even elevating them to intriguing works of art. I admire the deft way all have created inviting spaces within rooms, always making comfort a priority. And they have conceived outdoor spaces as enchanting as the interiors.

As for myself, I've been molded by many influences. As a child, I was shaped by our dear family friend Mrs. G and her remarkable Connecticut country house. Throughout my life I was shaped by my parents, who fostered my love for home and my passion for creating a beautiful, warm, and welcoming place for friends and family to gather. In my careers at Polo Ralph Lauren and Ethan Allen, my love of interior design, classic style, and innovative new ideas blossomed. And today I'm still learning from those who—like the homeowners featured here—show thoughtfulness, pride, and vision in their homes.

All of these opportunities and experiences shaped who I am and led to the aesthetics of my company, Nora Murphy Country House: a bestselling interior decorating book, a content-packed website, personal appearances, The Little Shop in Chester, Connecticut (my curated lifestyle shop filled with country house treasures), and now, this beautiful new book.

So, let me tell you a story. Or better yet, eight stories. Let the homes and homeowners in this book, each embodying the spirit of country house style, each enriched by a personalized point of view, share their tales.

EVERYTHING OLD IS NEW AGAIN

PREVIOUS PAGE: A French eighteenth-century painted cupboard is quite grand and is the focal point in Bill and Robb's garden house. It's thoughtfully packed with all things pastoral.
OPPOSITE: Chase and Stephenie brightened the second floor landing by painting the walls and floor white, showcasing the well-chosen pieces as art.

welcoming

In 2020, during the height of the pandemic, my family and I moved to a wonderful new (old) Connecticut country house—a feat in itself, to be sure! Many of you know the story of my previous country house from my first book, and just as with that one, I was not really looking for a new home when I found this next one.

My husband and I had come to realize that our beloved house in Newtown was becoming too burdensome for us to maintain. Alas, it was time to downsize. While we were just in the talking-about-it stage, a real estate ad on social media serendipitously caught my eye. It featured a stunning antique house in our favorite getaway town of Essex, Connecticut. Beautiful as that house was, it was a related home that truly piqued my interest—an 1820 historic Federal-style house nestled by the Connecticut River, with a front facade that was impeccably classic in style and color palette. I just knew that this smaller home and its postage-stamp-sized lot were the perfect next step for us.

A little backstory. Our family has been visiting the town of Essex for decades. From our previous house, it was just one hour's drive. We were captivated by the beautiful New England architecture, the river and the Gris, as the historic Griswold Inn is known.

And now, our new (old) house is right across the river from Essex! I remember walking my husband through the house for the first time and entering the large, empty room that was soon to be our bedroom. He gazed out the window and asked "Can you imagine waking up to this view every morning?" To which I answered quickly and emphatically, "Yes!"

This sublime house was lovingly restored with great care in the 1990s, yet what I loved most about it were its many features that defined country house style: the imperfections, like the wonky original floorboards and early

Samuel Brooks
1820

AMERICAN GARDENS

Southern Furniture 1680-1830
THE COLONIAL WILLIAMSBURG COLLECTION

JOHN DERIAN

wavy glass in the windows; the sense of light and connection to the outdoors through the large windows; the original details in the fireplaces and woodwork. And it was surrounded by similar antique homes, a historic ferry, a beautiful state park, and lovely, remarkably friendly neighbors. It checked all the boxes for the next chapter in our lives.

Because of its smaller size, I knew that only certain pieces could stay. Our former 1767 House in Newtown was close to 3,000 square feet, a thousand more than our new home. There were fewer rooms, with larger windows, so space was limited. Favorite finds needed to be functional as well as beautiful. Everything had to work harder and be even more special.

Ultimately, I wanted to add a freshness to this classic historic house in order to accentuate the sunlight that reflects off the river, drifts through our twelve-over-twelve windows, and casts our interior with beautiful brightness. So I painted all the walls, ceilings, doors, and trim with Benjamin Moore Super White, which perfectly complemented my creamy-white denim slipcovered upholstery. I added retractable shades only where needed—in the bedrooms for privacy and in the library/TV room for protection from the strong sunlight.

Sitting by the river, surrounded by woods, I wanted to bring the nature that surrounds this home indoors, where it seemed to want to be. I married coastal and forest through my collections, like the carved dining chairs that mimic branches. My cabinet of curiosities expanded with natural finds from our property. A large pair of framed garden plans set the tone for the front foyer, as well an antique pond boat.

Today, it is a remarkably inviting house, embracing friends and family who visit with warmth and coziness from the fireplaces and bringing smiles to their faces with its unique, unexpected touches. This is what I love about country house style—it creates happy, thoughtful environments.

MAKING AN ENTRANCE

PREVIOUS PAGES: The front foyer sets the tone for the whole house. Chippy Chinese Chippendale chairs with apron-style slipcovers are a natural fit here. OPPOSITE: I love gazing out our windows and watching sailboats, so when I spotted this pond yacht at one of my favorite antique shops, I had to have it. The gilded oval mirror over the eighteenth-century American faux-bois chest brings reflected light to a dark corner.

Country house
style is about
adding character
with all things
collected and found.

LOVINGLY CURATED

RIGHT: Two generously scaled
glass vessels contain my collection
of beachcombed shells, joined by
a handwoven hat from Madagascar
and a pair of chocolate-brown-
painted faux-wood ducks.

FOLLOWING PAGES: Generous
windows soak the living room in
glorious morning light. My cozy
upholstered pieces (including the
best napping sofa ever!) from my
former living room made their way
to this new one. Well-loved nautical
touches keep up the coastal spirit.

FRAME A VIEW

ABOVE: The living room's fireplace wall started with the antique oil painting of an esteemed gentleman and a pair of mirrored sconces. As the room evolved, I added favorite artwork, mostly old and some new, always keeping a balance in mind. **OPPOSITE:** The cabinet of curiosities that anchored my former home's entry serves the same purpose in this room. It's filled with an ever-growing collection of found and preserved items from nature that I and my family treasure.

PASSION FOR PLAID

LEFT: I've adored all things tartan since I was a child, so you can imagine how I reacted when I spotted this unique nineteenth-century Scottish tartan chest of drawers at Brimfield years ago. **OPPOSITE:** It's key to keep sightlines in mind when layering one-of-a-kind vintage items. Color, scale, pattern, and texture all come into play—and together create an impactful effect.

NORA'S NOTES
Coastal Touches

Try letting your location inspire your decorating. Sited near the Connecticut River with gardens and woods nearby, my house called for sea themes and nature. I love to display works by area artists and favorite finds from nearby getaways. Here are several coastal touches I've added to my living room that have made all the difference.

CLOCKWISE FROM TOP LEFT: An antique handcrafted boat adds weight and dimension to the corner, while a vintage toybox that once belonged to Chip, a nineteenth-century pastel portrait, and a framed vintage nautical flag form a colorful backdrop. A large glass jar filled with prized mementos nestled among delicate scalloped seashells sits where I can see it every day. The lemon-verbena nest from my sister, Judy, holds gifts from the sea. Souvenir miniature ships in a bottle add charm. A petite hooked rug from Mystic Seaport fit an old carved footrest frame I had stored away; my dear friend Lucia married the two by adding filler, gimp trim, and brass nailheads. The marine-themed all-in-one antique letter holder and inkwell was made in France.

Angelo Balestrino
CAPITANO MARITIMO
MEDAGLIA D'ORO PER LUNGA NAVIGAZIONE

A neutral
background allows
treasures to
stand out.

FORM AND FUNCTION

PREVIOUS PAGES: The living room's mantel is an open invitation to restyle with the seasons or the latest finds. **LEFT:** The Victorian seashell mirror is perfect for that spot in shape, size, and style. **OPPOSITE:** My friend Mike Tenk handcrafted the statement-making whale above the mantel. **FOLLOWING PAGES:** The dining room floor was a dark-stained oak. I took a leap of faith and painted it white. What a difference!

Black and white is
a classic pairing
that will never go
out of style.

A BOLD SILHOUETTE

LEFT AND OPPOSITE: Some things
stay with you wherever you go.
This wonderful, black-painted
serpentine wall shelf has always
been a natural match with the
coral collection that I started
years ago. A few sweet antique
transferware pieces have found
their way into the mix.

A country kitchen
is the perfect
antidote to a busy
working life.

RUSTIC ELEGANCE

I'd always dreamt of a kitchen
with a fireplace. This big beauty
is perfect for hearth cooking
and morning-into-evening fires.
Our old Irish pine farm table is a
natural fit and perfect for casual
gatherings. The beaded stained
wood walls were painted white
to brighten the cozy space.

SIMPLE CHARM

ABOVE AND OPPOSITE: My childhood home had a pantry, and I always loved the "nook" feel of it. This one houses all my dinnerware as well as a beloved menu written by Conor when he was five. **FOLLOWING PAGES, CLOCKWISE FROM TOP LEFT:** The mantel of the cooking fireplace has the luxury of length and surface to tell a maritime story. Flanking the antique diorama are a pair of brass anchor andirons and Richard Scofield custom sconces. The stove wall holds all good ingredients at hand. Fabulous foraged pieces by Bramble Collective freshen the windowsill. The cookbook library houses a pair of bay laurel topiaries, an antique French harvest basket, and the hand-painted lid of an early sailor's box.

EMBRACING HALLWAYS

ABOVE LEFT AND OPPOSITE: Eighteenth-century French engravings by François Martinet found the perfect home at the top of the stairs. **ABOVE RIGHT:** This sliver of a wall in the front hall packs quite a punch with Mary Maguire's giclee print housed in an antique folk-art ship-rope frame, Andy Teran's driftwood whales, and nineteenth-century oils. **FOLLOWING PAGES:** The breezy Cape Cod room (named after one of our favorite family getaways) keeps guests in a summer state of mind with wicker, Americana bedding, and nautical artwork.

For my bedroom,
I took inspiration
from the Connecticut
River outside our
windows and
introduced blues and
sea glass into the
creamy white palette.

RIVER VIEWS

**OPPOSITE, CLOCKWISE FROM TOP
LEFT:** The room that leads to our main
bedroom is a hardworking space—part
library, part TV-watching area. Details
from the primary bedroom. **RIGHT:** A
favorite montage includes my pastel
drawings from past Cape Cod getaways.
FOLLOWING PAGES: The weathered-
wood touches in the main bedroom
were inspired by Nantucket (another
favorite getaway). Ethan Allen's Quincy
bed anchors the room and faces the
river view. The large brick chimney
forms a handsome sightline with the
Bluenose, America's Cup ship.

KEEPING IT CLASSIC

ABOVE: The little path to the front gate is planted with fairy roses. **OPPOSITE:** Our old faux-wicker table and chairs served us well for many years in Newtown and now do the same in Hadlyme. Our southwestern patio is surrounded by stone walls, mature boxwood hedges, and a new perennial garden—as well as that beautiful view of the river.

CHAPTER 2

elegant

Everything about this couple, and this home, evokes a story. Stephenie and Chase shared a mutual affection for home design even as high school sweethearts. As teenagers, their dates often consisted of browsing the mall, fantasizing about owning their own home, and imagining how they would decorate it. Today, they head their own interior design studio, Watts Design House.

They found their Connecticut country house in a whirlwind. Early one morning at home in Utah, Chase was perusing Connecticut houses online. "I knew I wanted a historic home in Connecticut, and I didn't care where in the state it was," remembers Chase. When he came across the ad for this one, he roused Stephenie and told her, "You have to see this." "Great, I love it," she enthused, before drifting back to sleep.

That weekend they flew to Connecticut and immediately put in an offer. The following weekend they returned for the inspection. "We had never stepped foot in Connecticut before. When we arrived and saw the area, we looked at each other and marveled, 'Where are we?'"

Where they were is called the "Quiet Corner," a rural, wooded region in northeast Connecticut, tucked under the Massachusetts border. Much like the area, this remarkable house, a former tavern on the road from Providence to Hartford, is imbued with history.

Stephenie and Chase's country home dates back to 1802, though one of the most charming rooms, the summer kitchen, with its magnificent stone fireplace, originated in 1792. Before air-conditioning, homes often had summer kitchens, which were used for cooking, bathing, laundry, and canning and preserving garden produce, so that the rest of the house kept cool during the warmer months. The risk of fire was also reduced.

Stephenie and Chase are eager stewards, guiding their home into the present while respecting its history. And what history lives inside these walls: The original owner's family bible and register are displayed in the sitting room, along with a well-worn vintage "receiving chair." A tavern bill from 1835 hangs in an annex outside the taproom. The property also features a historic barn, the home's original privy, and a wellhouse with a chimney where lambs would go in winter to keep warm.

Inside, nine fireplaces and four sets of stairs add to the home's individuality. The original cage bar itself has been faithfully recreated. "A previous owner found parts of the bar in the attic," says a grateful Chase. "He even uncovered the original tavern owner's oil portrait, which now hangs above the fireplace. Incredibly, it was covered in wallpaper and had been used as a fireplace blocker!"

Throughout the house, the past is preserved. "We've never even added a new nail to the walls. Everything we've hung is on an existing peg, or where there was already a hole," reports Chase.

CHECKS, PLEASE
The house came with the hand-painted checkerboard floor that is a scene stealer from all sight lines. The exquisite pair of antique side chairs connect the graphic floor to the ornate gilded chandelier.

The bright, inviting living room was formerly the keeping room and served as a lobby where the inn's guests would congregate. It's also where cooking was done for taproom customers. Steel hooks where herbs, flowers, and spices hung to dry still drop from the ceiling.

"This was not called an inn, but people could stay here," recounts Chase. "Bedrooms had actual beds, or just ticking, depending on how much guests wanted to pay."

Favorite finds from nearby shops, flea markets, and the couple's extensive travels enhance each room. "Every place, every country I've visited has opened my eyes to something new about life and design," affirms Stephenie. Parisian and colonial influences and European inspiration abound, meshing seamlessly with the home's antiques and even its modern elements.

Stephenie and Chase, along with their two children, Klein and Hampton, have settled comfortably in this time-honored home, enjoying their country life filled with long walks, gardening, and home school. Stephenie and Chase are avid antiquers, and Hampton and Klein often join their parents on such jaunts.

"Owning an old home isn't always easy," Stephenie continues. "There are expenses, repairs, lots of crazy ups and downs. But just like life, old homes are full of love, memories, and joy."

CLASSICALLY DETAILED
PREVIOUS PAGES: With understatement and simplicity, the front parlor communicates beautifully that less is more. OPPOSITE: An empty antique frame invites attention to the graceful form of the Empire-style armchair.

STRONG SILHOUETTES

OPPOSITE AND ABOVE: Each item of furniture and accent piece stands on its own, and together they create an air of calm and elegance that is enhanced by the light palette. A large antique rug unites the seating areas.

FLICKERS OF THE PAST

OPPOSITE: In the dining room, the family lights candles every evening. The French mirrored wall sconces add reflected light. **RIGHT:** The cage taproom has been faithfully recreated. A previous owner found items from the bar in the attic, including the original tavern owner's oil portrait that now hangs above the fireplace. It had been covered in wallpaper and used as a fireplace blocker.

No matter how
sophisticated
the surroundings,
comfort is
fundamental.

A MODERN SENSIBILITY

RIGHT: The family room is
spare, but steeped in cushy
comfort. The slipcovers of the
upholstered pieces are easy
to launder, and the chocolate-
brown velvet oversize tufted
ottoman serves as an ad hoc
play area. **FOLLOWING PAGES:**
In the main bedroom, classic
English and French pieces
have enduring appeal. A pair of
vintage Chapman brass lamps
are a handsome touch and
anchor the bedside chests.

NORA'S NOTES

JUXTAPOSITIONS

Disparate styles in the same space can bring a modern element to a historic home and create a dramatic contrast. Chase and Stephenie's country house draws its power from the interplay between elegance and rusticity.

CLOCKWISE FROM TOP LEFT: The deck and seat cushions of an antique Chippendale-style wing chair are upholstered, but the back, wings, and arms show off the "bones" of this classic beauty. A Sheraton-style sofa is a true early nineteenth-century classic, and dressed in white linen it's elegant and understated at the same time. A vintage tray allows everyday items to be organized and layered atop favorite books, while a chic rectangular seagrass tray serves as the foundation. Jute braided trim is stunning on classic white linen drapery panels. Stephenie's slippers have style. Fanciful trim adds a soulful touch to this well-loved antique footstool.

In an old house, history can be the most pivotal design element.

BEAUTIFUL BORDERS

OPPOSITE AND RIGHT: The stencil in the dressing room was recreated by the former owner, who uncovered a small piece of the eighteenth-century original in a corner above one of the doors. The grand nineteenth-century mirror, cupboard, dressing table, and French settee romanticize the period feel.

BEHIND CLOSED DOORS

OPPOSITE: In the primary bath, a William and Mary–style dresser holds towels and other necessities.
ABOVE: The former owners left a pair of hardworking custom cabinets housing sinks and vanities that provide ample but hidden storage.

SWEET DREAMS

ABOVE: Hampton's dreamy bedroom is pretty, but sophisticated enough to suit her as she grows. A vintage quilted floral settee contrasts with a modern gilded flower-form table and botanical prints simply framed in gold. **OPPOSITE:** The Shaker-style rope canopy bed is anchored by a pair of painted chests of drawers and opaque lamps.

Thoughtful
details help a
child's bedroom
grow with them.

CHILD'S PLAY

OPPOSITE AND RIGHT: Hampton
and Klein often join their
parents on antiquing jaunts.
Klein's room mixes some of
their unique finds with kid
favorites like dinosaur models
and stuffed animals.

Old houses grow
more beautiful
with age, filled
with the memories
of the families
who have lived
within their walls.

STORYTELLERS

LEFT: The centuries-old summer kitchen's fireplace is graced with touches from long ago, including a found handwritten recipe for pumpkin and squash pie.
OPPOSITE: Quiet moments that seem to exist out of time, from antique rippled glass panes to a single nail holding a calico apron.
FOLLOWING PAGES: The original summer kitchen is not insulated or heated, but it is bursting with historical charm, and is soon to be the new location for the family's new kitchen.

AUTUMN IN NEW ENGLAND

ABOVE: The deep putty color of the old house shows off its classic features. **OPPOSITE:** A side door that leads to the summer kitchen is the family's go-to entrance, and everyone participates in decorating it for the seasons.

joyful

How does a former government analyst end up living in a newly built cottage on the coast of Maine that appears as if it's always been there? "I was looking for a diamond in the rough, a piece of rock that would reveal a diamond," Molly remembers. Boy, did she ever find one!

"After retiring, I needed a lifeline. A place that spoke to me," says Molly, who went to college in New Hampshire. She fell in love with the natural beauty of Maine when two of her children attended college in the state, and she decided to explore properties there. Molly knew she didn't want to be "in the boonies," preferring instead to be near a town and cultural opportunities. Most important, she wanted a home close to the water.

Her find? Two 1950s motor inns that weren't even winterized on a waterfront lot in an isolated cove. But Molly saw beyond the rundown buildings to what was really there: a beautiful field, a lawn, a marsh, and then a magnificent water view. She could envision a new home in that space, with that view. A place for everyone to gather, play games, and reminisce. And did I mention the view? It's a commanding, ever-changing vista, thanks to weather and tides.

So, the transformation began. First, Molly fully renovated the smaller upper building, converting it to a cozy guest cottage. Then came the real work; completely razing the waterfront home and lovingly designing an updated coastal cottage.

The new house offers a panoramic view of the sea that's visible the instant you walk in the front door. While the house is new, touches like beadboard

ceilings and pine beams enhance its old feel. And the center fireplace between the living and dining rooms was constructed with stones unearthed from the property, providing a link to the place and its past. The house exudes coastal Maine charm and is a testament to Molly's love of interior design, casual living, and the color blue.

Molly comes from a family of collectors, and she laughingly admits she is "not a minimalist." She traveled with her grandparents on antiquing adventures both in the United States and in Europe. She inherited her mom's love of blue-and-white transferware, and today she owns a staggering, museum-quality collection. She is grateful (and lucky!) to live close to the nexus of Maine's remarkable antiquing scene and auctions.

While Molly has no professional interior design training, she is fascinated by design and knows what she likes: color and pattern—especially on whimsically painted antique furniture, which can be found throughout the house.

A HOUSE FOR ALL SEASONS

PREVIOUS PAGES: The meadowed path to the front door of the cottage. **OPPOSITE:** Molly's welcoming entrance, beautifully infused with Maine's simple charm and hardiness. **ABOVE:** The bungalow-inspired architecture suits the seaside locale.

In true country house style spirit, Molly wants her house's soul to be one of old Maine, evident in an antique map of the state hanging beside the entry stairwell and the bounty of books, prints, and paintings by local artists and authors.

Yes, there are places for favorite things, and she layers her collections throughout the house. Of course, when your home sits on a spit of land jutting into a cove, a seafaring theme is likely to prevail. So, vintage fish molds float across the kitchen. A bucket of oars sits in a hallway. In the dining room, a school of fish-patterned plates swim down a wall, and a fleet of ship-shaped doorstops sail underneath.

Then there are the pieces that have extra meaning, like the treasured sailors' valentines hanging over her bed, painstakingly handcrafted with the tiniest of shells. Along with the mirror gifted to her by her children, they evoke memories of family vacations in Nantucket.

In a setting like this, it's only natural that the country house spirit extends to the outdoors as well. The wraparound deck is ringed with limelight hydrangeas, inviting you to kick back and enjoy the amazing view. A pair of Adirondack chairs await on the field below, and there are kayaks at the ready.

For Molly, the house is a cozy haven where she's able to "come in and put my feet up." Her children are grown and married, and her husband spends the majority of his work time in California. She dreams of handing the house down to her children, so they can continue the family traditions there.

In the meantime, Molly, her dogs, Maddie and Cisco, and her cats revel in this home that is full of wonder, bathed in natural light, and an endless source of views. She is close to town, with its lively community of lobstering, artists, galleries, and museums. Living here embodies Maine's state slogan: "The way life should be."

HOMEY CHARM
The focal point of the entrance alcove is a nineteenth-century chest painted in a faux-wood grain, topped and surrounded by antique picnic boxes and buckets. In a small space, stacking is definitely encouraged.

A breezy palette of
blue and white is the
perfect complement
to a coastal setting.

DARK MEETS LIGHT

LEFT: The antique English
credenza is a family heirloom
that acts as a bold anchor in the
center hallway and the heart of
the house and contrasts with
the airy living room ahead.
OPPOSITE: Vintage swivel
chairs in front of the stone
fireplace are slipcovered to add
to the breezy feel, as well as
to accommodate Maddie and
Cisco, Molly's springer spaniels.

Cherish old
things: they have
a history and
their own stories.

PATTERN PLAY

PREVIOUS PAGES: There's a
sense of whimsy in the living
room thanks to the mix of
patterns and motifs. Molly
changes slipcovers seasonally,
but sticking to a classic blue-
and-white color combination
creates a consistent look
year-round. **OPPOSITE AND
RIGHT:** Seashells in all their
different guises add interest
and texture, as does an old
nautical book. In this case,
more is definitely more!

NORA'S NOTES
THE WONDER
OF WHIMSY

There's a distinct, personal feel to the collections of delightful things found throughout Molly's home. Wonderfully worn collected pieces play well together, and add vintage charm and warmth.

CLOCKWISE FROM TOP LEFT: Small-scale, one-of-a-kind antique chairs can add historic appeal to an empty spot, and they bring so many styling opportunities. A collection of hand-carved and hand-painted shorebirds invites the beauty of nature indoors and adds sculptural interest to Molly's coastal style. I love the unexpected way the vintage fish plates swim up the wall above a simple bar setup! A collection of antique painted cast-iron ship doorstops sail across the base of a petite hand-painted Victorian chest. The monkey fist lamp, in style and scale, connects the two collections. The corner cupboard in Molly's dining room is filled with beautiful vintage blue-and-white spongeware bowls that rest atop one another. Amassing the collections into large bowls and baskets makes a strong statement. And when a collection gets too large to display, why not stack? (Molly's secret: place a small plastic container between the bowls to separate them and show off more of each bowl's inherent beauty.) Molly's collection of seashells is quite prolific!

SMART NAUTICAL

PAGES 98-99 AND PREVIOUS PAGES: The inviting dining area is a natural gathering place for family. It is open to the kitchen and to a wraparound deck for effortless entertaining. **ABOVE:** The kitchen has an appealing relaxed practicality. **RIGHT:** A creative composition of fish plates, platters, and molds.

Whimsically painted antique furniture often tells a story or starts a conversation.

LOCAL TREASURES

LEFT: The second-floor landing is dressed with graphic found pieces that contrast with the blue-painted walls. An antique pine barrel holds a collection of timeworn oars, all sourced locally. **OPPOSITE:** Different moods coexist in this guest bedroom. An armada of stately ships surround a vintage mariner's portrait, while on the chinoiserie night table a vintage lamp sports a playful sailor-boy base.

Sailors' valentines
from the nineteenth
century were
painstakingly
handcrafted with
the tiniest of shells
and brought home
to loved ones.

A SUNNY DISPOSITION

OPPOSITE: The elements on the headboard were part of a set Molly found at a nearby antique store, and she added posts to create a queen bed. From the beachcombed whelk shell finials to the pattern play of the bedding, Molly keeps it whimsical. **RIGHT**: A cherished collection of antique wicker in a palette of blue and white is as sweet as it is practical.

A mix of blues—navy, aquamarine, slate, and robin's egg—echo the sea and sky just outside the windows.

BATH TIME

RIGHT: The mudroom/laundry room handles muddy feet and paws with a custom-built dog shower and plenty of storage. **OPPOSITE, CLOCKWISE FROM TOP LEFT:** Molly's main bath is wallpapered in custom inky blue-and-white maps of her cove. Navy blue keeps the bath feeling crisp. Washable slipcovers—and that convenient dog shower—mean dogs can be welcomed onto the furniture. Vintage wooden cobbler's molds are reimagined as handy towel holders in the pups' shower. **FOLLOWING PAGES:** The expansive wraparound deck is a favorite spot to relax, take in the view, and enjoy the good life.

CHAPTER 4

soulful

Tina grew up in western New York a few miles from Lake Erie, the same area where she lives today with her husband and children. When Tina and her husband saw their current house, it was priced out of their range. But they submitted a low offer, the seller came down in price, and Tina's dreams of having an old house to love and fix up were suddenly a reality.

The house had been through a lot. It had been converted into separate apartments, then renovated back into a single-family home. Tina said that it was hard to tell what the original house was like, but they have done their best to create spaces that work for their family today.

The first ten years the couple spent in the house were dedicated to raising babies and doing strictly necessary updates. "So much paint," says Tina. "And there was that one cracked plaster ceiling that decided to crash right down on our heads!" Once the kids were older, they were able to undertake larger renovations to the bathrooms, kitchen, and laundry room, all of which were completed over the last seven years.

Tina doesn't consider her old Victorian home, with its period bones and trim, a country house, but that doesn't stop her from cultivating a country feeling. All of her favorite styles are here: cottage, vintage, farmhouse, antique. But for Tina, nothing works unless it translates to cozy, inviting, welcoming, lived in, and functional.

Charm seeps out of every nook and cranny of this home. Wooden floors add warmth to a white kitchen; a sliding barn door does the same for the white primary bedroom, where a great crystal chandelier adds dazzle. The whole house brims with examples of classic design with a startlingly fresh approach.

Thrifting, estate sales, yard sales, the internet—if Tina sees something she likes, she finds a spot for it. No requirements, no themes, just a penchant for European style, primitive and antique pieces, linen, and all things comfortable. Tina doesn't amass collections of particular items. "I collect lots of different things that fall under the same category—old stuff!" Tina inherited found treasures from her mom, an ace garage-sale shopper. Once embarrassed by her mom "digging through bins of other people's old stuff," Tina now stops at every sale she sees.

She notes that she only has one hard-and-fast rule, which is to decorate "without spending a ton of money." Then she laughs and admits, "Okay, except maybe for the occasional French antique." But surely that fabulous tapestry scrolling down the living room wall is an incredible find from a trip to Italy. "No," Tina shrugs. "I got it at a clearance sale at a local furniture store. I liked it and figured I'd be able to use it somewhere."

Tina grew up in a rustic old farmhouse, and country living and country houses are in her bones. While she might not have the farmhouse she always thought she would, she's adept at creating family-centric and friend-welcoming coziness in her village home. She and her family love everything small-town life has to offer; there's even a village park with a bandshell right across the street!

Tradition, finding favorite things, and working with what you have—it's all part of country house style.

ALL IN THE MIX
The foyer of Tina's nineteenth-century house is both grand and welcoming. The elegant high ceiling, staircase, and crystal chandelier are balanced by the more rustic unfinished banister, old wicker trunk, and Victorian coatrack.

REFINED FARMHOUSE

LEFT AND OPPOSITE: The living room's exposed brick fireplace and the dining room's uncovered beams lend a modern, loft-like feeling. Tina painted the dining room's old cupboard—originally light in color—a rich black to add punctuation to the surroundings. **FOLLOWING PAGES:** Her impressive collection of vintage ironstone and treenware is displayed artfully in the cupboard, calling to mind an old master still life.

DEPTH, DRAMA AND FLOW

ABOVE: The rich black finish of the vintage piano and cupboard add depth to the space.
OPPOSITE: Tina found the dramatic landscape canvas at a favorite shop and got it for a song!
It is scaled perfectly to the big comfy sectional that is the gathering place for their family
of six. **FOLLOWING PAGES:** All the rooms on the main floor have an open feeling and easy flow.

KITCHEN CHARMS

ABOVE: Tina grew up in an old farmhouse, so country living is in her bones. She even cans tomatoes in the hardworking open kitchen that is perfect for a busy family. **OPPOSITE:** An antique general store cabinet is reimagined as the kitchen's coffee bar. Vintage items on the wall contribute days-gone-by charm as well as modern-day use.

PERFECTLY COMPOSED

ABOVE AND OPPOSITE: Even though the library is located in the heart of Tina's bustling home, it is an intimate space with a peaceful vibe. The painted walls are hand-rubbed to add depth. Pillows and textural throws add comfort to the vintage settee and chair. Natural wood pieces and the cowhide rug bring butterscotch-hued warmth to this sweet space.

RUSTIC ROMANTICISM

OPPOSITE: The neutral palette of the main bedroom suite highlights the collected wall grouping that Tina created with vintage bits and pieces. The bed could only be placed in this asymmetrical position, partially blocking one window. The weight of the grouping casts the windows in a secondary role, bringing balance to the space. **ABOVE:** An oversize barn door slides open to reveal the main bath lined in white tile and shiplap. **FOLLOWING PAGES:** A room fit for princesses is fitted with a pair of antique French caned twin beds that Tina painstakingly stripped.

When workspaces
feel luxurious, taking
care of a home
becomes a pleasure.

HOME COMFORTS

LEFT: A wood-burning
stove paired with a comfy
chair and ottoman make
Tina's dream laundry room/
mudroom the ultimate
escape. **OPPOSITE:** A hand-
painted checkerboard floor
leads to the girls' bathroom,
complete with an antique
sliding door. No need to
enclose the shelving niche—
seagrass baskets keep
storage looking stylish.

NORA'S NOTES
STORAGE STYLE

Storage in a laundry room/mudroom never looked so good, or camera ready. Tina's collection of all things rustic has a visual consistency, from sun hats and a newer handwoven tote to a vintage fishing creel and sculptural rug beater. A handcrafted wall shelf complete with brackets holds stacked picnic baskets that are not only stylish but are clever storage solutions. The vintage iron hooks are staggered on its backboard and keep smaller items handy, from a whisk broom to a dog leash. Fishing poles in the corner add vertical visual interest and connect the antique hardware chest of drawers that holds small bits and pieces to the wall grouping. Note the handmade peg rack for drying and storing boots. Brilliant!

CHAPTER 5

timeless

"There are a lot of centuries in my home," remarks designer and milliner James Coviello with a smile. Indeed, entering this reverently restored treasure in New York's Hudson Valley is like stepping back in time. It is an eloquently composed love letter to the nineteenth-century art, architecture, and romanticism that have captivated James since childhood.

For James, this deep appreciation for times past and affection for the stories and history behind objects began with his "hunt-obsessed" parents. His father, a graphic designer, and his mother, whom James describes as "extravagantly European," brought James along to auctions, estate sales, flea markets, shops, and museums. During annual visits to his mother's native Switzerland, they would pack into their rented car and embark on antiquing adventures to Geneva, Zermatt, Basel, Venice and beyond. Fast-forward to a day trip years later to Olana, the nineteenth-century Middle Eastern–inspired home of Hudson River School artist Frederic Church. Its interior, a beautiful

example of the Aesthetic movement, with its florals, stencils, tassels, and calligraphy, spoke to James, as did the surrounding landscape. "Immediately, I knew the Hudson Valley was where I wanted to be," remembers James. "And I knew the kind of home I wanted."

The criteria for his house search included finding something that remained in as close to its original state and as architecturally untouched as possible. "I was looking for a home that still had timeworn features like molding and mantels and plaster walls and old floors," he remembers. "And I knew I wanted land, as long as it was a scale I could physically and financially take care of." And he definitely wanted to be in the country, but not too far from a town. After a few years of searching (and saving), he found his 1840s Greek Revival country home, a place James lovingly refers to as "perfectly imperfect." Says James, "It was owned by a shoemaker, and I've really strived to maintain its authenticity."

Today, much like Olana, the house is an ode to the 1800s Aesthetic movement that embraced beauty in all its forms. The look is simultaneously stylized and worldly. Vintage details dominate. Crystals hang from Victorian candleholders. Fanciful Old Paris porcelain vases line the pantry shelves. Antique lamps and light fixtures, elaborately framed mirrors, and Staffordshire figures define each room.

Like most country house dwellers, James is a collector. He's a connoisseur of curiosities, enamored of reminders of days gone by. A series of cuckoo clocks adorn a bedroom wall. "I found the box of all twelve cuckoo clocks for ten dollars at a local shop. They were mostly parts," James proudly recalls.

A DELICATE BALANCE

PREVIOUS PAGES: A vintage industrial worktable-cum-firewood caddy pairs unexpectedly yet quite beautifully with vine-patterned wallpaper. I love the interplay of the elegant chinoiserie and figurine lamps with the rough-hewn shelf. A pair of Hudson River School views complete the wall. **OPPOSITE:** The commanding scale of the living room's mantel is balanced by the nineteenth-century gilded mirror and layered Victoriana above.

Not much about the house is new, and most everything James finds, he uses. When he came across a mantel in the barn, he restored it and enlarged it to fit the fireplace in the parlor. He added architecturally matching bookcases.

Like all great country homes, James's house is defined by its owner's influences. His fashion designer's eye shapes his preferences for patterns, texture, color, and sentiment. To satisfy his passion for studying and learning about the past, he frequents historic houses and gardens and visits decorative arts museums whenever he travels.

James's love of nineteenth-century novels—his shelves are lined with the works of Zola, Proust, Balzac, Wilde, and Flaubert—informs the authentic, romantic feeling he creates. He's especially enamored with the authors' descriptions of the routines of daily life, the homes and rooms the characters lived and breathed in.

"I'm an idealist, I'm nostalgic, I'm an aesthete," says James. "Right now, this is my art—designing my house, tending my garden, entertaining my guests. Most importantly, doing it all in a home where I live happily today with the look, mood, and spirit of yesterday."

What I most admire about James and his approach to the past is that the house does not feel like a museum. It is lived in. It's a home where 150-year-old plates are used for dining, not just display. Vibrant needlepoint pillows add warmth to vintage sofas. And a turn-of-the-twentieth-century cupboard and worktable take on modern kitchen duties. There is no better way to pay homage to the past.

EMBRACING THE PAST
PREVIOUS PAGES: The art, furnishings, and architecture of the interior are an ode to the 1800s Aesthetic movement that embraced beauty in all its forms. Tufted-back settees and chairs—a pair of each—are perfectly scaled to the room. OPPOSITE AND FOLLOWING PAGES: In the dining room, nineteenth-century pieces add romantic touches. Wall sconces are crafted from Victorian funeral flowers that were once staked in the ground. An antique mirror and cut-crystal candelabras add sparkle against ocher-colored walls.

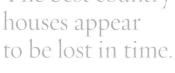

The best country
houses appear
to be lost in time.

QUIET BEAUTY

OPPOSITE AND RIGHT: The rustic
fixtures in the old pantry express a
humble utilitarian look, especially
the antique cast-iron enamel
sink that James uses for flower
arranging. A collection of Old Paris
porcelain vases line a pantry shelf.

FOLLOWING PAGES: The kitchen
ceiling was lifted. Cabinets were
replaced with found and unfitted
cupboards, and the walls were lined
with beadboard. Exhaustive sanding
of the floor revealed beautiful aged
blue paint underneath.

NORA'S NOTES
FUNCTIONAL TREASURES

For James, naturally aged elements, softly faded facades, and clever reimagining are all attributes of a well-loved home. Country house style embraces the idea of using favorite items every day to further develop their patina and history.

CLOCKWISE FROM TOP LEFT: Stand-alone kitchen cupboards and cabinets, like this hard-toiling turn-of-the-century beauty with its original robin's-egg blue paint, make up for the lack of built-ins. Check out the window "valance" of antique copper pots. Rust, wear, and patina pay homage to the history of a vintage drawer handle, all part of what James lovingly describes as "decadent decay." James's recipe for stylish entertaining: find one perfectly primitive chalkboard at a very good price, jot favorite cocktail mixes on it, and embellish with hawk feathers discovered in the garden. The intricately engraved glass panel on an upcycled antique clock case resembles a veil of Victorian lace. James creatively repurposed the clock case as a small hanging curio cabinet, perfect for displaying some of his favorite Staffordshire littles! Proof of James's tenet that beautiful pieces should be used and not just put on display, these colorful Chinese bowls and hand-painted ceramic tile "place mats" provide haute meal settings for Maurice, his shih tzu.

THE NARRATIVE OF HOME

ABOVE: Every part of James's country house tells a story. Selections from his collection of nineteenth-century gilded mirrors adorn the second-floor hallway, juxtaposed with a soft and nostalgic wallpaper he chose and an assemblage of antique mounted antlers. **OPPOSITE:** The path from the primary bedroom across the hall to the primary bath is layered with worn Persian rugs.

A SENSE OF ADVENTURE

PREVIOUS PAGES: The primary bedroom features an antique spool bed with a time-honored crewel coverlet. **ABOVE:** A pair of early splat-back chairs anchor a wall grouping that includes framed Hudson River School vistas. **OPPOSITE:** The turn-of-the-last-century folding screen was once used to display wallpaper samples for sale. **FOLLOWING PAGES:** A Chinese screen behind an antique cannonball bed makes the tiny guest bedroom simultaneously stylized and worldly.

PERFECTLY IMPERFECT

ABOVE: Hidden beneath floral wallpaper in the guest bedroom were original, unpainted plaster walls.
James left pieces of the vintage paper to meld with the plaster's hue. "It's imperfect, it's rough, and
it's beautiful," he says. **OPPOSITE:** "I found the box of all twelve cuckoo clocks for ten dollars at a local shop.
They were mostly parts," James proudly recalls.

graceful

For over thirty years, Marta and I have been the dearest of friends and, at times, colleagues and creative partners. I have long admired her fine yet understated style and distinctive approach.

Marta's home is a unique variation on a new old house, and she refers to it as "a shipwright's fancy." She commissioned the beautiful bow house, built in 1983, to be a faithful reproduction of the Jabez Wilder house in Hingham, Massachusetts, circa 1690. Like its inspiration, Marta's main house has a bowed or rainbow roof that resembles the curved hull of a ship and readily sheds rain and snow. The accompanying saltbox was added in 1996.

"I love capes and saltboxes. To me, all the basic elements have very pure proportions, with a timeless quality and simple beauty," remarks Marta.

Bow House (the company) reproduced the Jabez Wilder House, and Marta worked with their architect to customize it. "I loved so much about the design of this house," says Marta. "The bowed roof, which actually gives more space upstairs than a regular cape, the overall architectural simplicity and pure design."

Unique details stand out, like the wide fascia and corner boards, and the graduated clapboard on the front, mirroring a ship's hull. The builders gathered everything on the interior and exterior: hand-cast brick, blown glass, authentic iron hardware, wide board floors, hand-planed raised-panel doors and millwork. "Remember, this was all before the ease of online shopping," remembers Marta, "so it was much more difficult to cull all of these materials then."

Marta's house is steeped in historically appropriate features. The four fireplaces are classic Rumford designs, with beveled brick and hearth tiles. The house is bathed in sunlight and shares the property with a wildflower meadow.

Everything flows seamlessly here. For example, the dining room, with its fireplace and round table, segues to a raised bluestone patio. Even the wall treatments add a natural tone to the home. Marta says, "I love the simulated whitewash because the nuances and textures change as the light moves. Repainting and touch-ups only add more character, and the raked painting technique gives the illusion of aged horsehair plaster."

The same thoughtful approach extends to practical items. "When it was time to select plumbing and heating fixtures, I kept everything simple, classic, and in scale with the house, so those choices would harmonize with

THE POWER OF RESTRAINT

ABOVE: Marta's love of historic New England houses brought her to seek out period architectural plans for her Bow House; the new addition is to the right. **OPPOSITE:** Simple, eloquent touches abound on the exterior, including the striking brass clamshell door knocker on the coal-black door, the trained ivy embracing old steppingstones, and the zinc planters deftly potted with triple topiaries and petunias.

the colonial design," remembers Marta. But that doesn't translate into outright mimicry or reproduction. Instead, she says, "I like combining different elements, so they look modern and fresh." This approach is skillfully rendered in the kitchen, where the stainless sink and appliances juxtapose dramatically with painted cabinets, soapstone countertops, and primitive decor. "Overall, I tend to avoid trends," Marta continues. "And that has helped me appreciate the choices I made back when the house was built. The kitchen's handmade ballast brick floor is a great example. It's simple and rustic, and I still love it today."

Marta considers lighting critical, and in true country house style each fixture has a story. Many of them were handcrafted by the late Richard Scofield, founder of Period Lighting Fixtures in Chester, Connecticut. Explains Marta, "The chandelier in the kitchen was originally designed for a ship's cabin. The centerpiece was weighted with sand to ensure balance and keep it from pitching side to side in turbulent seas."

Marta's design expertise is reflected in the subtle details of her home, like the gold-leaf detailing she had an artist add to a meetinghouse chandelier with graceful arms that hangs in the dining room and to the sconces that flank a highboy in the primary bedroom. Marta says, "He used 22-karat gold leaf, and then the gilding was muted with an antique glaze."

Marta is a patient, measured collector. "I am more of a minimalist than most collectors. I rotate things to change the look and feel of a room and keep things new and current. I love eighteenth-century design and natural curiosities."

Spare, muted, stately, cultivated: Marta's home embodies the beauty of keeping it simple.

WELL-WORN BEAUTY
PREVIOUS PAGES: The family room features a soft palette of putty, cocoa, and sea glass. OPPOSITE: An eighteenth-century New England pantry cupboard with its original drying rack anchors the dining area. FOLLOWING PAGES: At the front entrance, a generous Guy Wolff pot filled with rosemary rests on an antique demilune table. The hand-painted checkerboard floor adds early farmhouse appeal (left). In the family room, the eighteenth-century reproduction cupboard handcrafted by Bryce Ritter conceals the TV (right).

A quiet palette
inspires
contemplation.

CLASSIC REVIVAL

PREVIOUS PAGES: The original
1983 kitchen was updated
to include state-of-the-art
appliances (including a wine
fridge) while keeping with the
aesthetic of the rest of the
house—repainted cabinets, new
charcoal soapstone counters,
and a deep stainless steel sink.
On the left, an old painted plate
rack holds Marta's treenware
plates, charcoal porcelain, and
petrified-wood cheese boards.
LEFT: The early farmhouse
open step back cupboard
filled with Marta's extensive
collection of Guy Wolff pottery
is the punctuation in the dining
room. **OPPOSITE:** Well-chosen
kitchen details complete the
farmhouse look. **FOLLOWING
PAGES:** In the dining room, the
generously scaled reproduction
meetinghouse chandelier with
graceful arms and exquisite
gold-leaf detail was custom-
made by Richard Scofield.

Natural elements
connect a
country house
to the world
outside its windows.

LIVING WITH GRACE

PREVIOUS PAGES: To suit the cozy scale of the living room, Marta chose a pair of Ethan Allen camelback settees with custom-made cotton duck slipcovers for seating. An Early American–inspired tea table anchors the grouping. **LEFT:** An antique find, the eighteenth-century painted corner cupboard is filled with old coral. It inspired the color of the room's paneled fireplace wall and trim. **OPPOSITE:** An antique Federal gilded mirror with *verre églomisé* hangs over a reproduction eighteenth-century demilune table that Marta restyles seasonally.

HONORING SIMPLICITY

RIGHT: To update the main bedroom, the Eldred Wheeler custom canopy bed was stripped and stained in an ebony tint so that the tiger maple grain would remain visible. New bedding from Ethan Allen and Les Indiennes adds a modern freshness.

FOLLOWING PAGES: A creamy white background allows antique gilded finds from a Paris flea market to stand out. The classic Ethan Allen highboy is topped with an exquisite centuries-old bandbox found at Brimfield.

REFINEMENT AND ROMANCE

OPPOSITE AND ABOVE: The only wallpaper in the house is in the primary bathroom, and it was chosen because it reminded Marta of the type used to cover bandboxes in the early nineteenth century. Marta asked the late Kolene Spicher, an artist she greatly admired, to create the framed ship painting that hangs over the tub. "I sent her a shard of wallpaper and Pantone chips, plus an early silverleaf frame I'd had for years. It arrived complete with antique wavy glass and blends beautifully with the paper."

Bringing the Inside Out

Marta puts the same attention and work into the exterior as she does the interior. Every detail is elegant, yet measured and understated. Repeating motifs, such as the white Drift® roses that are used throughout, make the space feel curated, but never fussy. An outdoor shower (inspired by annual getaways on Nantucket) and comfortable furniture are practical touches. This is indoor-outdoor living that truly flows.

CLOCKWISE FROM TOP LEFT: At the home's side entrance, white Drift® roses—miniature shrubs that love sun and add enchantment to a garden—are surrounded by a boxwood knot garden and a backdrop of climbing hydrangea. A sun-bleached teak picnic table and benches are set off by a pair of metal Windsor armchairs. The fully functional steel marine-grade shower is fenced and has a bluestone floor; a large clamshell holds a bar of soap. A pair of white Drift® rose topiary standards in gray clay pots flank the back door. The zinc planters feature a spiral boxwood topiary with underplantings of white cosmos, white verbena, dusty miller, black magic petunia, and white lobelia.

FOLLOWING PAGES: A checkerboard of bluestone squares adds visual interest to the grassy lawn; a row of black Adirondack chairs face south to catch the best rays.

artful

A Chesterfield sofa designed to accommodate not only the two homeowners but their four excitable, inquisitive greyhounds as well is surely a testament to how welcoming their house is! And the greyhounds run in the family: Collin's great-grandparents raised the breed, loving their athleticism and demeanor.

"We tend to move once a house reaches a point of completion. A new old house allows me to explore different design directions," says Collin, an interior designer. Their current house was built in 1722, a typical colonial farmhouse. A two-floor addition in 1805 made the home a bit more stately with a front-to-back entrance foyer, parlor, library, two upstairs bedrooms and bathrooms, and four additional fireplaces. The rural Connecticut area where they live is beginning to grow and transition into a town.

Collin often refers to himself as an "environmental designer," and he strives to create an atmosphere. "I enjoy searching for a narrative, seeing how the overall, not just the details, affects the finished vision." For Hound House, they envisioned an English country home crossed with a hunting lodge.

While it's Collin who generally takes the lead on design initiatives, Trent readily offers his opinions and thoughts, and he acts as a sounding board for Collin's creativity. In their years together, both of their tastes have changed and rubbed off on each other. "Collin used to be much more modern," says Trent.

I admire so many things about their style. There are high contrasts throughout, and opposites definitely attract. Black meets white, new joins rustic, dark walls provide a dramatic backdrop for curated pieces and curios. Imperfect items, like a paint-chipped cabinet or distressed floor, cozy up to more recent, pristine pieces. "They bring out the best in one another," says Collin. "We want you to walk through the house and feel like you're on an adventure. I love finding items that get people talking—things that might at first seem odd or even controversial."

A CREATIVE REFUGE

ABOVE: Perched on a hill, surrounded by mature trees and gardens, the center of the Federal-style home dates back to 1772, while a "new" addition was built in 1805.
OPPOSITE: In place of a traditional door, an ornately trimmed drapery panel entices visitors to peek into the library, drawing the eye to Collin and Trent's imaginative book display.

Displaying collections pays homage to the people who created the items and allows the pieces—and portrait subjects—to live on.

PLAIN AND SIMPLE

In the library, to maintain Shaker-like simplicity, Trent covered every book in plain brown paper, and Collin handwrote the title on each spine. The books set off the deep blue walls, and provide a suitable backdrop for the early nineteenth-century portrait.

Walking through
a house packed
with curios means
noticing something
new every time.

THE INSIDE STORY

LEFT: The living room is the most
bold and masculine room in
the house. Decorative objects,
including the affectionately
named Wentworth the goat, are
silhouetted against dark walls.
**OPPOSITE, CLOCKWISE FROM
TOP LEFT:** Both Collin and Trent
are attracted to the imperfect,
such as the library's antique
leather club chair. Collin likes to
start dramatic groupings with
a dominant item, like the large
mantel clock from their favorite
antiques dealer, DC Kingswood,
then develop a mood with other
pieces. The powder room off
the library is an artful blend of
antique materials: copper, brass,
iron, marble. In the living room,
a vintage iron garden chair cozies
up to an antique secretary.

NORA'S NOTES

A Passion for Collecting

Collin and Trent believe that "collections find us, one way or another." Begin to amass your own groupings of vintage objects, personal mementos, natural finds, and other items that catch your eye and share a common thread.

Horns, antlers, and turtle shells are all about form and texture . The magnifying glass, tool of the naturalist, fits right in with them. Vintage photographs relay family heritage, inspire memories, or simply add visual interest. Leatherbound or not, antique books can be displayed for their age-old beauty or used as risers supporting curiosities. Collin and Trent are awed by nests, feathers, and eggs and their patterns and hues.

BE OUR GUEST

ABOVE AND OPPOSITE: Collin and Trent love to entertain by candlelight and firelight, so the hearth room (the original kitchen) is a prime spot for cocktails and conversation. The original cooking fireplace is the focal point of the room, and all the seating gathers around the hearth. The antique wing chair was reupholstered in an unconventional material: vintage US mailbags! **FOLLOWING PAGES:** The kitchen is painted with Studio Green from Farrow & Ball. I love the pop of rich red from the old Turkish rug.

Collin and Trent love to find the drama in a home, the vignette in a room. Every corner, every shelf, every room here tells a story in a magical, fun, even eccentric way. These are tales of style—and memories. Everything is meaningful; each souvenir harkens back to a specific moment in their lives, from a Texas childhood to a favorite vacation in Louisiana to their time living in Manhattan. "Collin has a great ability to tell a story, our story," affirms Trent.

There's also an unmistakable air of humor and whimsy about many of their collections, like a menagerie of, yes, vintage taxidermy. "I get a lot of design ideas and style sense from nature," says Collin. "The color of a bird's breast, the design on a feather, the texture and pattern on a leaf, the shape of a nest."

Trent confirms, "Collin is obsessed with birds, nests, and eggs. Flora and fauna offer him an endless array of design elements and style directions."

Looking at a favorite framed photo of his great-grandfather and grandfather with a pack of greyhounds, Collin notes that there's reverence in the house, too. "Whether it's our stuffed animals, our collection of oil portraits, or our family treasures, our space offers an opportunity for us to honor the artists and subjects, and they can take on new lives here," he explains.

Collin and Trent's country house has provided them with something they reference often: the incredible feeling of being exactly where they are supposed to be—a chance to savor moments that pass by too quickly.

PORTRAIT GALLERY
The visual weight of this vignette derives from the paintings. The two antique portraits on the lower right and left are hand-painted tintype photos from Collin and Trent's very first Brimfield trip and have been boldly matted and framed. The faux-leopard velvet pillow and hand-stenciled zebra-striped cowhide provide fresh contrast.

Rich patterns
and handsome
fabrics create
warmth and a
sense of
contentment.

CLASSICALLY DETAILED

OPPOSITE: Collin referenced his
English heritage for the main
bedroom, located in the oldest
part of the house, by utilizing
classic pieces and motifs,
from the scalloped wooden
canopy, bed hangings, and
upholstered headboard to the
broken-in leather Chesterfield
sofa. **RIGHT:** The dressing room
is the epitome of charm, with
a window seat and an antique
iron-pedestal table. **FOLLOWING
PAGES:** The British flag and
Scottish sporran are a nod to
Collin's heritage. The couple's
use of black paint for the
walls allows the commanding
presence of the nineteenth-
century military portrait to pop
and be the focus of the room.

CHAPTER 8

pastoral

Long before we met, Bill and Robb and I knew each other through magazine articles, my blog, and social media. When my family and I moved to our new country house, we were thrilled to discover that Bill and Robb's property, River Road Farm, was just up the road.

Two decades ago, Bill and Robb were living and working in Georgia, where Bill is from. But their hearts were set on relocating to Robb's home state of Connecticut and the countryside there that they both loved. For two years they made the sixteen-hour drive back and forth, looking for an old home, something they could put their imprint on.

A fortuitous meeting with two real estate agents led them to River Road Farm, and the instant they saw the house, they knew it was the one. The property presented a blank slate. The house itself, sitting in the middle of a field, was a clean palette to work with. Here they could create a garden from scratch, not inherit someone else's vision.

Better still, the town and surrounding area reminded them both of the places where they had grown up, filled with mom-and-pop businesses that had everything they could possibly need.

Were they up for transforming eleven bare acres and renovating a house? A daunting task for sure, but as one of Bill and Robb's favorite sayings goes,

"Just like a turtle, you only make progress if you stick your neck out." Is it any wonder their home is dotted with displays of found turtle shells?

The white clapboard house, a 1732 center-chimney Colonial, had been added on to over the years, which contributes to its quirky charm. "Cozy rooms, low ceilings, and every room serves a purpose," says Bill, "like the book-lined snuggery off the kitchen, a perfect place to relax, especially in winter, with a fire blazing in the fireplace and something delicious in the oven for dinner."

But what about those early years when the couple split their time between Connecticut and Georgia? "Surprisingly, it worked to our advantage," remembers Robb. "Being away, coming back, that distance afforded us the opportunity to evaluate everything we were doing with fresh eyes."

A SOURCE OF JOY

PREVIOUS PAGES: River Road Farm features a 1732 center-chimney Colonial, along with four outbuildings and glorious cultivated gardens on eleven acres. **ABOVE:** The barn is located next to the house and is surrounded by multiple mini gardens, including an espalier of the Cox's orange pippin apple, which was one of Thomas Jefferson's favorites. **OPPOSITE:** The snuggery is a cozy library in the heart of the house where Bill and Robb spend most of their winter hours.

Nothing is overly modern inside, and everything carries the patina of history and stories. There's a touch of formality to their style, yet Bill and Robb have brilliantly made it a cozy formality, one that opens their home to friends and says, "Welcome."

Happily, it is a place made to showcase tradition. Robb and Bill have been antiquing for years, and also inherited many beloved pieces from family. There is now a home for all of it: Robb's mother's garden tools rest in the warming shed. His family's tall case clock rings in childhood memories every time it chimes. A sink that once belonged to a revered garden conservator is now a fixture in the potting shed.

If there's a mantra in this home, it's "Always have a view of the garden." The magnificent gardens are showstoppers, with surprises and color at every turn. Part Georgian Revival, part English cottage, it is astonishing how they relate to and complement the house.

Formally structured with casual plantings, the landscape is dotted with structures. A warming shed off the barn houses plants in winter. A studio for garden planning is set back from the actual gardens, so you don't think of weeding and hoeing while creating. And a bit of a walk away, perched on a hill, is what Bill and Robb laughingly refer to as "the temple," a unique gathering place dedicated to appreciating serenity, the four seasons, friendship, dining, and entertaining.

To Bill and Robb, country house style is about the rhythm of a home. Slight renovations are permissible, as long as they evince respect for the past. The history of an admired antique, a recollection sparked by a cherished heirloom—these are core elements. Their version of the style is always alive, forever moving—the garden constantly changing, views seen with fresh eyes, purple finches returning to nest, everything flowing from season to season. It's the love in a home that makes it grand.

PALETTE PLAY

PREVIOUS PAGES: In the living room, a comfy roll-arm sofa and a pair of vintage butterscotch leather club chairs converse with a red chinoiserie coffee table piled with favorite books. A Welsh dresser behind the sofa showcases a charming collection of English Staffordshire pottery and Portuguese majolica. **OPPOSITE:** Continental antiques unite with Provençal red-and-white gingham.

A SENSE OF OCCASION

PREVIOUS PAGES: The dining room is dressed in Bill's favorite, blue and white. The Hepplewhite period table and Hepplewhite-style chairs, Continental furniture, gilded nineteenth-century mirror, and formal window treatments are grounded by a loomed dhurrie rug. **ABOVE:** The nineteenth-century mahogany sideboard belonged to Bill's grandmother and is the perfect foundation for the couple's wall grouping of willow and Staffordshire ware. **OPPOSITE:** Fanciful hand-etched hurricanes with starburst and laurel-wreath motifs were a long-ago Christmas gift from Bill and Robb to Bill's late mom and add classical style (as well as sparkle) to the dining room table.

A room is most successful when you enter it and know exactly what it's all about.

SUNNY-SIDE UP

OPPOSITE: A stately concrete turtle greets visitors as they enter the garden room. Three walls of windows ensure this space is bright and cheerful. The skirted table (one of a pair) was specially constructed to bear the weight of a lamp made from a concrete garden flower basket. The graceful red tea table is from the estate of Bunny Mellon. **RIGHT:** A floor-to-ceiling library wall houses Bill and Robb's extensive collection of garden books. The petite house portrait was painted by the couple's dear friend, Tom Rose.

Decorative objects themselves are only part of the equation. The history and remembrances that those items represent put the soul in a home.

GOOD INGREDIENTS

PREVIOUS PAGES: The English-inspired country kitchen is large in scale, but it is made cozy with charming decorative touches, including antique Persian scatter rugs on the terra-cotta-tiled floor and a mix of pendant lighting fixtures and table lamps.
LEFT: The kitchen table is kept orderly under the watchful eye of the antique Staffordshire gardener on a catch-all inlaid sherry tray that holds beloved pieces like the antique English saltcellar and pepper grinder with sterling silver bands. **OPPOSITE:** Bill and Robb fell in love with the color of the antique wall shelf they found in England, brought it back home, and naturally filled it with English Staffordshire and ironstone.

DETAILS MATTER

ABOVE, LEFT: The walls of the main bedroom are upholstered in a sand-hued woven linen that sets off the wood tone of this nineteenth-century linen press. **ABOVE, RIGHT:** I love a pillow with a good sense of humor! **OPPOSITE:** The Gustavian-style staircase landing features a bust of Thomas Jefferson. **FOLLOWING PAGES:** The tiger-maple four-poster bed is simply dressed in fine white-cotton linens. Balanced styling brings out the best in the nineteenth-century silhouettes flanking the gilded bull's-eye mirror. The classic gourd lamps are by Bill and Robb's friend, Christopher Spitzmiller.

BE OUR GUEST

ABOVE: In one of the two guest bedrooms presides the first bed Bill purchased as an adult, a Shaker-style canopy he bought from his parents' furniture store. The architectural engravings are from the Firestone estate in Grosse Point, Michigan. **OPPOSITE, CLOCKWISE FROM TOP LEFT:** An Edwardian settee frames antlers collected on trips to England. An inexpensive cherry highboy was transformed into a work of art with hand-painted chinoiserie by local artist Tom Rose of Black Whale Antiques. A charming collection of miniature salesman samples from Bill's parents' century-old furniture business, located in his hometown of Newnan, Georgia.

Decorating with
family heirlooms
enriches a home
with reminders
of the past to enjoy
every day.

A VERDANT VIEW

LEFT: The green bedroom is lined in vintage toile de jouy fabric that belonged to Bill's mom. It's the perfect backdrop for Robb's Louis XV chest of drawers, a masterpiece of marquetry with a flower basket motif. **OPPOSITE:** The early nineteenth-century Empire daybed features Bill's favorite pattern—checks. The pillow was hand-painted by George Oakes and was originally a custom gift from Mario Buatta to a friend. **FOLLOWING PAGES:** Bill was on a ladder cleaning the back windows of the house when he turned around and took in the incredible view of the gardens—and the idea of this classic southern porch was born. It's the perfect spot to begin the day with a cup of coffee and end it with a glass of wine.

NORA'S NOTES

Quiet Moments and Seasonal Joys

"Life begins the day you start a garden," says an old Chinese proverb. Planning an entire garden at once can be overwhelming. Instead, pick a starting point and expand from there. Bill and Robb began with a fountain and an arbor, then went on to create places to sit, paths, and birdhouses on their eleven acres of land.

CLOCKWISE FROM TOP LEFT: Lush Boston ivy is the backdrop to an old wire plant stand—a place to host green and flowering guests in mossy pots. White wire benches are strategically placed throughout the garden for resting and taking in the view. This white arbor and the urn fountain in the distance were the starting points for Bill and Robb's extensive garden. An old Lutyens bench anchors the space. A potager planted with cabbages and other vegetables and edged with woven willow fencing is situated close to the house for easy access. The path to and from the house passes under the arbor.

Don't be limited by walls. Home can extend to the garden and beyond.

A GARDENER'S DREAM

LEFT: The garden house is located on level ground behind the perennial garden. **OPPOSITE:** Woven grass bee skeps speak to Bill and Robb's love of pollinators. The antique painted trunk was a gift from Bill's dad, and the watering can belonged to renowned interior designer William Hodgins and reads, "A present for William." It was gifted to Bill. **FOLLOWING PAGES:** An open hand represents opportunities (and this one holds a freshly picked Meyer lemon). An antique southern school teacher's desk is equipped for all kinds of projects.

acknowledgments

As in my first book, I must start by thanking my now 95-year-old mom, Charlotte, for introducing me to my very first country house, and to my late dad, John, who taught me to work hard at all things—especially what I'm passionate about.

Thank you to my fantastic family: my husband, Rick; our son, Conor; my sister, Judy; and my sisters and brother from other mothers, Suzy, Holly, Aida, Carol, Lucia, and Dave, for always believing in me and supporting me in all that I set out to do.

To Stephenie and Chase, Molly, Tina, Collin and Trent, James, Marta, Bill and Robb: Thank you so very much for saying yes to us taking over your beloved country houses for a couple of days and allowing us to show the beauty and care you put into your homes.

To my wonderful literary agent, Dana Newman: You have believed in me since day one and I look forward to making many more books together!

Thank you to my dear friends, the Nora Murphy Country House dream team: Carol Hubner, gifted art director, you are my anchor; DuAnne Simon, photographer extraordinaire, you always capture the magic; John Simon, accomplished co-writer, you are such a good listener and storyteller; Kimberley, Colleen, and Lucia from The Little Shop, you jumped right in and worked so hard to help me get my country house camera-ready!

Thank you to the Rizzoli dream team: Charles Miers, publisher, for seeing the beauty in *Country House Living* and wanting to add it to the Rizzoli library; Kathleen Jayes, senior editor, your thoughtful work and guidance kept us true to the vision of making this book the best it can be; Doug Turshen and David Huang, book designers, your design work makes each country house feel so classically elegant, yet personal; Natalie Danford, copyeditor; Kaija Markoe, production manager, and Lynn Scrabis, managing editor, your hard work made this book a reality.

To my Nora Murphy Country House readers, friends, fans, followers and community: Your loyalty and lovely spirit truly inspire me, and I am forever grateful to you all. Thank you.

First published in the United States of America in 2024 by
Rizzoli International Publications, Inc.
300 Park Avenue South
New York, NY 10010
www.rizzoliusa.com

Copyright © 2024 Nora Murphy
Text: John Simon
Photos: DuAnne Simon

Publisher: Charles Miers
Senior Editor: Kathleen Jayes
Design: Doug Turshen with David Huang
Production Manager: Kaija Markoe
Managing Editor: Lynn Scrabis

Printed in China

2024 2025 2026 2027 / 10 9 8 7 6 5 4 3 2 1

ISBN: 978-0-8478-9979-1

Library of Congress Control Number: 2023946868

Visit us online:
Facebook.com/RizzoliNewYork
Twitter: @Rizzoli_Books
Instagram.com/RizzoliBooks
Pinterest.com/RizzoliBooks
Youtube.com/user/RizzoliNY
Issuu.com/Rizzoli